For Beginners Workbook

Learn The Most Commonly Used Words In Context

Ibrahim Musa

TABLE OF CONTENTS

Introduction

Hi!

This book was written to help beginners pick up the most common Arabic words that are used in day-to-day life. This book will cover a wide range of vocabulary, each word will include the plural. I will also allow you to practice writing each word, as you will be able to trace it and then write it yourself a few times after that. Each word will also have a sentence with it, to help you grasp how to use that word in the correct context.

Learning Arabic can be a gruesome task, especially with boring material. This book has been created to make your experience fun and lasting.

Be sure to take your time through this workbook, and try your hardest to memorise every word and verb in this book, as it will take you one step closer to becoming fluent in the Arabic language.

Furthermore, please pay close attention to how words are used in sentences. If a word has multiple sentences, this means that it can be used in a variety of contexts, please take note of this and be well aware of it.

☆ Important note

You will see in this book that the masculine version of a singular and plural noun is used for the majority of examples, as this is the standard of the Arabic language.

For example, one of the words in the last chapter was "بَخِيلٌ" which translates to "cheap/greedy" However, if you wanted to change these nouns and adjectives to the feminine singular, you would simply add ة at the end of the word. So, the word would now become بَخِيلَةٌ.

If you wanted to turn the feminine singular into the feminine plural, you would add ات at the end of the word. So, the word would now become بَخِيلات

In the examples where the singular of a word has a ة at the end of the word, this is an indication that the word is feminine and does not have a masculine version. For example, أَرِيْكَةٌ is the singular of "Sofa". This is a singular word that is feminine in its nature. There will also be a few of these words in this book that you will come across.

Another important thing to note is that some of the nouns/adjectives in this book have multiple plurals, however, the most common one was used in this book, so if you do come across another plural for a word, do consider that, please.

Chapter 1: Around The House

① بَيْتٌ
House

Singular (مُفْرَدٌ)	بَيْتٌ	بَيْتٌ	بَيْتٌ	بَيْتٌ
Plural (جَمْعٌ)	بُيُوتٌ	بُيُوتٌ	بُيُوتٌ	بُيُوتٌ

Sentence

رَجَعْتُ اِلَى الْبَيْتِ بَعْدَ الْمَدْرَسَةِ

I returned home after school

Write your own sentence below!

شَقَّةٌ
Flat/Apartment

Singular (مُفْرَدٌ)	شَقَّةٌ	شَقَّةٌ	شَقَّةٌ	شَقَّةٌ
Plural (جَمْعٌ)	شُقَقٌ	شُقَقٌ	شُقَقٌ	شُقَقٌ

Sentence

اِشْتَرَيْتُ الشَّقَّةَ يَوْمَ الخَمِيسِ

I purchased the flat on Thursday

Write your own sentence below!

3

بَابٌ
Door

Singular (مُفْرَدٌ)	بَابٌ	بَابٌ	بَابٌ	بَابٌ
Plural (جَمْعٌ)	أَبْوَابٌ	أَبْوَابٌ	أَبْوَابٌ	أَبْوَابٌ

Sentence

اِفْتَحْ الْبَابَ بِهُدُوْءٍ

Open the door quietly

Write your own sentence below!

مِفْتَاحٌ
Key

| Singular (مُفْرَدٌ) | مِفْتَاحٌ | مِفْتَاحٌ | مِفْتَاحٌ | مِفْتَاحٌ |
| Plural (جَمْعٌ) | مَفَاتِيْحُ | مَفَاتِيْحُ | مَفَاتِيْحُ | مَفَاتِيْحُ |

Sentence

لَا تَنْسَى الْمِفْتَاحَ لَاحِقًا

Don't forget the keys later

Write your own sentence below!

5

جِدَارٌ
Wall

Singular (مُفْرَدٌ)	جِدَارٌ	جِدَارٌ	جِدَارٌ	جِدَارٌ
Plural (جَمْعٌ)	جُدُرٌ	جُدُرٌ	جُدُرٌ	جُدُرٌ

Sentence

هَلْ نَرْسُمُ الْجِدَارَ بِاللَّوْنِ الْأَزْرَقِ؟

Shall we paint the wall blue?

Write your own sentence below!

سَطْحٌ
Ceiling

Singular (مُفْرَدٌ)	سَطْحٌ	سَطْحٌ	سَطْحٌ	سَطْحٌ
Plural (جَمْعٌ)	سُطُوْحٌ	سُطُوْحٌ	سُطُوْحٌ	سُطُوْحٌ

Sentence

لَا تَتَسَلَّقَ السَّطْحَ!

Don't climb the roof!

Write your own sentence below!

كَهْرَبَاء
Electricity

Singular (مُفْرَد)	كَهْرَبَاء	كَهْرَبَاء	كَهْرَبَاء	كَهْرَبَاء

Sentence

قَلِّلْ مِنْ اِسْتِخْدَامَكَ لِلْكَهْرَبَاء

Limit your use of the electricity

Write your own sentence below!

8

جَارٌ
Neighbor

Singular (مُفْرَدٌ)	جَارٌ	جَارٌ	جَارٌ	جَارٌ
Plural (جَمْعٌ)	جَيْرَانٌ	جِيرَانٌ	جِيرَانٌ	جِيرَانٌ

Sentence

عَامِلْ جَيْرَانَكَ بِاحْتِرَامٍ

Treat your neighbors with respect

Write your own sentence below!

غُرْفَة
Room

Singular (مُفْرَدٌ)	غُرْفَةٌ	غُرْفَةٌ	غُرْفَةٌ	غُرْفَةٌ
Plural (جَمْعٌ)	غُرَفٌ	غُرَفٌ	غُرَفٌ	غُرَفٌ

Sentence

نَظِّفْ غُرْفَتَكَ قَبْلَ أَنْ تُغَادِرَ

Clean your room before you go

Write your own sentence below!

مَمَرٌّ
Corridor

Singular (مُفْرَدٌ)	مَمَرٌّ	مَمَرٌّ	مَمَرٌّ	مَمَرٌّ
Plural (جَمْعٌ)	مَمَرَّاتٌ	مَمَرَّاتٌ	مَمَرَّاتٌ	مَمَرَّاتٌ

Sentence

كَانَ الأَوْلَادُ يَتَسَابَقُوْنَ فِي المَمَرِّ

The boys were racing down the corridor

Write your own sentence below!

12

11

أَثَاثٌ
Furniture

Singular (مُفْرَد)	أَثَاثٌ	أَثَاثٌ	أَثَاثٌ	أَثَاثٌ
Plural (جَمْع)	أَثَاثَاتٌ	أَثَاثَاتٌ	أَثَاثَاتٌ	أَثَاثَاتٌ

Sentence

كَانَ الأَثَاثُ بَاهِظُ الثَّمَنِ لِلْغَايَةِ

The furniture was very expensive

Write your own sentence below!

13

كُرْسِي
Chair

| Singular (مُفْرَد) | كُرْسِي | كُرْسِي | كُرْسِي | كُرْسِي |
| Plural (جَمْع) | گَرَاسِي | گَرَاسِي | گَرَاسِي | گَرَاسِي |

Sentence

سَقَطَ الصَّبِيُّ مِنْ كُرْسِيهِ فِي الصَّفِّ

The boy fell off his chair in class

Write your own sentence below!

13

أَرِيكَةٌ
Sofa

Singular (مُفْرَدٌ)	أَرِيكَةٌ	أَرِيكَةٌ	أَرِيكَةٌ	أَرِيكَةٌ
Plural (جَمْعٌ)	أَرَائِكُ	أَرَائِكُ	أَرَائِكُ	أَرَائِكُ

Sentence

نِمْتُ عَلَى الأَرِيكَةِ بِالأَمْسِ

I slept on the sofa yesterday

Write your own sentence below!

طَاوِلَةٌ
Table

Singular (مُفْرَدٌ)	طَاوِلَةٌ	طَاوِلَةٌ	طَاوِلَةٌ	طَاوِلَةٌ	طَاوِلَةٌ
Plural (جَمْعٌ)	طَاوِلَاتٌ	طَاوِلَاتٌ	طَاوِلَاتٌ	طَاوِلَاتٌ	طَاوِلَاتٌ

Sentence

سَقَطَتْ نَظَارَتِي الشَّمْسِيَّةِ مِنْ الطَاوِلَةِ

My sunglasses fell off the table

Write your own sentence below!

نَافِذَةٌ
Window

Singular (مُفْرَدٌ)	نَافِذَةٌ	نَافِذَةٌ	نَافِذَةٌ	نَافِذَةٌ
Plural (جَمْعٌ)	نَوَافِذُ	نَوَافِذُ	نَوَافِذُ	نَوَافِذُ

Sentence

قَفَزَ القِطُّ مِنْ النَافِذَةِ

The cat jumped out the window

Write your own sentence below!

تِلْفَازٌ
Television

Singular (مُفْرَدٌ)	تِلْفَازٌ	تِلْفَازٌ	تِلْفَازٌ	تِلْفَازٌ	تِلْفَازٌ
Plural (جَمْعٌ)	تِلْفَازَات	تِلْفَازَات	تِلْفَازَات	تِلْفَازَات	تِلْفَازَات

Sentence

تَرَكَتْ إِمِيلِي التِّلْفَازَ مَفْتُوحًا

Emily left the TV open

Write your own sentence below!

هَاتِفٌ
Telephone

Singular (مُفْرَدٌ)	هَاتِفٌ	هَاتِفٌ	هَاتِفٌ	هَاتِفٌ
Plural (جَمْعٌ)	هَوَاتِفُ	هَوَاتِفُ	هَوَاتِفُ	هَوَاتِفُ

Sentence

تَتَأَكَّدْ مِنْ ضَبْطِ الْمُنَبِّهِ عَلَى هَاتِفِكَ لِلْمَدْرَسَةِ

Make sure to set the alarm on your phone for school

Write your own sentence below!

18

مِصْبَاحٌ
Lamp

Singular (مُفْرَدٌ)	مِصْبَاحٌ	مِصْبَاحٌ	مِصْبَاحٌ	مِصْبَاحٌ
Plural (جَمْعٌ)	مَصَابِيْحُ	مَصَابِيْحُ	مَصَابِيْحُ	مَصَابِيْحُ

Sentence

هَلْ لَدَيْكَ مِصْبَاحٌ فِي غُرْفَتِكَ؟

Do you have a lamp in your room?

Write your own sentence below!

19

سَجَّادَةٌ
Carpet

Singular (مُفْرَدٌ)	سَجَّادَةٌ	سَجَّادَةٌ	سَجَّادَةٌ	سَجَّادَةٌ	
Plural (جَمْعٌ)	سَجَّادَاتٌ	سَجَّادَاتٌ	سَجَّادَاتٌ	سَجَّادَاتٌ	

Sentence

لَا تَمْشِي بِحِذَائِكَ عَلَى السَّجَّادَةِ

Don't walk with your shoes on the carpet

Write your own sentence below!

مِرْوَحَةٌ
Fan

Singular (مُفْرَدٌ)	مِرْوَحَةٌ	مِرْوَحَةٌ	مِرْوَحَةٌ	مِرْوَحَةٌ
Plural (جَمْعٌ)	مَرَاوِحُ	مَرَاوِحُ	مَرَاوِحُ	مَرَاوِحُ

Sentence

أَسْتَخْدِمُ المِرْوَحَةَ كَثِيرًا فِي الصَيْفِ

I use the fan a lot in the summer

Write your own sentence below!

مِمْسَحَةٌ
Mop

Singular (مُفْرَدٌ)	مِمْسَحَةٌ	مِمْسَحَةٌ	مِمْسَحَةٌ	مِمْسَحَةٌ	مِمْسَحَةٌ
Plural (جَمْعٌ)	مَمَاسِحُ	مَمَاسِحُ	مَمَاسِحُ	مَمَاسِحُ	مَمَاسِحُ

Sentence

أَنَا لا أُحِبُّ مَسْحَ الأَرْضِ

I don't like mopping the floor

Write your own sentence below!

بَطَّانِيَةٌ
Blanket

Singular (مُفْرَد)	بَطَّانِيَةٌ	بَطَّانِيَة	بَطَّانِيَة	بَطَّانِيَة	بَطَّانِيَة
Plural (جَمْع)	بَطَّاطِينُ	بَطَّاطِين	بَطَّاطِين	بَطَّاطِين	بَطَّاطِين

Sentence

أَنَامُ بِدُوْنِ بَطَّانِيَةٍ

I sleep without a blanket

Write your own sentence below!

سَرِيرٌ
Bed

Singular (مُفْرَد)	سَرِيرٌ	سَرِيرٌ	سَرِيرٌ	سَرِيرٌ	سَرِيرٌ
Plural (جَمْع)	سَرَايِر	سَرَايِر	سَرَايِر	سَرَايِر	سَرَايِر

Sentence

يَجِبُ أَنْ يَكُونَ السَّرِيرُ مَرِيحًا لِلْنَوْمِ فِيهِ

The bed should be comfortable to sleep in

Write your own sentence below!

وِسَادَةٌ
Pillow

Singular (مُفْرَدٌ)	وِسَادَةٌ	وِسَادَةٌ	وِسَادَةٌ	وِسَادَةٌ
Plural (جَمْعٌ)	وِسَادَات	وِسَادَات	وِسَادَات	وِسَادَات

Sentence

يَحِبُّ بِنْ النَوْمَ بِوِسَادَتَينِ

Ben likes to sleep with two pillows

Write your own sentence below!

خِزَانَةٌ
Closet/wardrobe

Singular (مُفْرَدٌ)	خِزَانَةٌ	خِزَانَةٌ	خِزَانَةٌ	خِزَانَةٌ	خِزَانَةٌ
Plural (جَمْعٌ)	خَزَائِنُ	خَزَائِنُ	خَزَائِنُ	خَزَائِنُ	خَزَائِنُ

Sentence

عَلِّقْ مَلَابِسَكَ فِي خِزَانَةِ المَلَابِسِ

Hang up your clothes in the wardrobe

Write your own sentence below!

مِرآةٌ
Mirror

Singular (مُفْرَدٌ)	مِرآةٌ	مِرآةٌ	مِرآةٌ	مِرآةٌ
Plural (جَمْعٌ)	مَرايَا	مَرايَا	مَرايَا	مَرايَا

Sentence

لِمَاذَا لَدَيْكَ مِرآةٌ فِي غُرْفَةِ الجُلُوْسِ؟

Why do you have a mirror in the living room?

Write your own sentence below!

مَكْتَبٌ
Desk

Singular (مُفْرَدٌ)	مَكْتَبٌ	مَكْتَبٌ	مَكْتَبٌ	مَكْتَبٌ	مَكْتَبٌ
Plural (جَمْعٌ)	مَكَاتِبُ	مَكَاتِبُ	مَكَاتِبُ	مَكَاتِبُ	مَكَاتِبُ

Sentence

أَقُوْمُ بِوَاجِبَاتِي عَلَى مَكْتَبِي

I do my homework on my desk

Write your own sentence below!

رَفٌّ
Shelf

Singular (مُفْرَدٌ)	رَفٌّ	رَفٌّ	رَفٌّ	رَفٌّ
Plural (جَمْعٌ)	رُفُوفٌ	رُفُوفٌ	رُفُوفٌ	رُفُوفٌ

Sentence

أَحْتَفِظُ بِكُتُبِي المُفَضَّلَةِ عَلَى الرَّفِّ الأَعْلَى

I keep my favorite books on the top shelf

Write your own sentence below!

مِشْطُ
Comb

Singular (مُفْرَد)	مِشْطُ	مِشْطُ	مِشْطُ	مِشْطُ
Plural (جَمْع)	أَمْشَاطُ	أَمْشَاطُ	أَمْشَاطُ	أَمْشَاطُ

Sentence

أَمْشُطُ شَعَرِي فِي الصَّبَاحِ قَبْلَ المَدْرَسَةِ

I comb my hair every morning before school

Write your own sentence below!

30

حَمَّامٌ
Bathroom

Singular (مُفْرَد)	حَمَّامٌ	حَمَّام	حَمَّام	حَمَّام
Plural (جَمْع)	حَمَّامَاتٌ	حَمَّامَات	حَمَّامَات	حَمَّامَات

Sentence

أَسْتَخْدِمُ الْحَمَّامَ كَثِيرًا طِوَالُ الْيَوْمِ

I use the bathroom often throughout the day

Write your own sentence below!

مِنْشَفَةٌ
Towel

Singular (مُفْرَدٌ)	مِنْشَفَةٌ	مِنْشَفَةٌ	مِنْشَفَةٌ	مِنْشَفَةٌ	مِنْشَفَةٌ
Plural (جَمْعٌ)	مَنَاشِفُ	مَنَاشِفُ	مَنَاشِفُ	مَنَاشِفُ	مَنَاشِفُ

Sentence

مِنَ الْمُهِمِّ غَسْلِ الْمِنْشَفَةِ كُلَّ أُسْبُوعٍ

It's important to wash your towel every week

Write your own sentence below!

صَابُونٌ
Soap

Singular (مُفْرَدٌ)	صَابُونٌ	صَابُونٌ	صَابُونٌ	صَابُونٌ
Plural (جَمْعٌ)	صَابُونَاتٌ	صَابُونَاتٌ	صَابُونَاتٌ	صَابُونَاتٌ

Sentence

أَنَا أُحِبُّ رَائِحَةَ الصَّابُونَ الْخَاصَّ بِكَ!

I like the fragrance of your soap!

Write your own sentence below!

33

مِكْوَاةٌ
Iron

Singular (مُفْرَدٌ)	مِكْوَاةٌ	مِكْوَاة	مِكْوَاة	مِكْوَاة
Plural (جَمْعٌ)	مَكَاوٍ	مَكَاوٍ	مَكَاوٍ	مَكَاوٍ

Sentence

عَمَلِيَّةُ كَيِّ الْمَلَابِسِ مُتْعِبَةٌ

Ironing clothes is tiring

Note – كَيّ is the verbal noun in this sentence, the act of "ironing"

Write your own sentence below!

مَطْبَخٌ
Kitchen

Singular (مُفْرَدٌ)	مَطْبَخٌ	مطبخ	مطبخ	مطبخ
Plural (جَمْعٌ)	مَطَابِخُ	مطابخ	مطابخ	مطابخ

Sentence

المَطْبَخُ مُتَّسِخٌ، نَظِّفْهُ مِنْ فَضْلِكَ

The kitchen is dirty, clean it please

Write your own sentence below!

ثَلَّاجَةٌ
Fridge

Singular (مُفْرَدٌ)	ثَلَّاجَةٌ	ثَلَّاجَةٌ	ثَلَّاجَةٌ	ثَلَّاجَةٌ
Plural (جَمْعٌ)	ثَلَّاجَاتٌ	ثَلَّاجَاتٌ	ثَلَّاجَاتٌ	ثَلَّاجَاتٌ

Sentence

أَغْلِقِ الثَّلَّاجَةَ بَعْدَ اِسْتِخدَامِهَا

Close the fridge after using it

Write your own sentence below!

مِطْرَقَةٌ
Hammer

| Singular (مُفْرَد) | مِطْرَقَةٌ | مِطْرَقَةٌ | مِطْرَقَةٌ | مِطْرَقَةٌ |
| Plural (جَمْع) | مَطَارِقُ | مَطَارِقُ | مَطَارِقُ | مَطَارِقُ |

Sentence

كُنْ مُنْتَبِهًا مَعَ الْمِطْرَقَةِ

Be careful with the hammer

Write your own sentence below!

مِلْعَقَةٌ
Spoon

Singular (مُفْرَدٌ)	مِلْعَقَةٌ	مِلْعَقَةٌ	مِلْعَقَةٌ	مِلْعَقَةٌ
Plural (جَمْعٌ)	مَلَاعِقُ	مَلَاعِقُ	مَلَاعِقُ	مَلَاعِقُ

Sentence

هَلْ تَأْكُلُ بِالْيَدِّ أَمْ بِالْمِلْعَقَةِ؟

Do you eat by hands, or by spoon

Write your own sentence below!

سِكِّيْنٌ
Knife

Singular (مُفْرَدٌ)	سِكِّيْنٌ	سِكِّيْنٌ	سِكِّيْنٌ	سِكِّيْنٌ
Plural (جَمْعٌ)	سَكَاكِيْنُ	سَكَاكِيْنُ	سَكَاكِيْنُ	سَكَاكِيْنُ

Sentence

لَا تَجْرَحْ نَفْسَكَ بِالسِّكِّيْنِ

Don't cut yourself with the knife

Write your own sentence below!

كُوْبٌ
Cup

| Singular (مُفْرَدٌ) | كُوْبٌ | كُوْبٌ | كُوْبٌ | كُوْبٌ |
| Plural (جَمْعٌ) | أَكْوَابٌ | أَكْوَابٌ | أَكْوَابٌ | أَكْوَابٌ |

Sentence

اِمْلَأْ كُوْبَكَ بِالْحَلِيبِ

Fill your cup with Milk

Write your own sentence below!

زُجَاجَةٌ
Bottle

Singular (مُفْرَدٌ)	زُجَاجَةٌ	زُجَاجَة	زُجَاجَة	زُجَاجَة	زُجَاجَة
Plural (جَمْعٌ)	زُجَاجَاتٌ	زُجَاجَات	زُجَاجَات	زُجَاجَات	زُجَاجَات

Sentence

اِحْمِلْ زُجَاجَةَ مَاءٍ عِنْدَ مُمَارَسَةِ الرِّيَاضَةِ!

Carry a water bottle when exercising

Write your own sentence below!

(41) مَدِيْنَةٌ
City

Singular (مُفْرَد)	مَدِيْنَةٌ	مَدِيْنَةٌ	مَدِيْنَةٌ	مَدِيْنَةٌ
Plural (جَمْعٌ)	مُدُنٌ	مُدُنٌ	مُدُنٌ	مُدُنٌ

Sentence

مَا هِيَ مَدِيْنَتُكَ المُفَضَّلَةِ فِي العَالَمِ؟

What is your favorite city in the world?

Write your own sentence below!

عِمَارَةٌ
Building

Singular (مُفْرَدٌ)	عِمَارَةٌ	عِمَارَةٌ	عِمَارَةٌ	عِمَارَةٌ
Plural (جَمْعٌ)	عِمَارَاتٌ	عِمَارَاتٌ	عِمَارَاتٌ	عِمَارَاتٌ

Sentence

اُنْظُرْ إِلَى تِلْكَ العِمَارَةَ الطويلةَ!

Look at that tall building!

Write your own sentence below!

شَارِعٌ
Street

Singular (مُفْرَدٌ)	شَارِعٌ	شَارِعٌ	شَارِعٌ	شَارِعٌ	شَارِعٌ
Plural (جَمْعٌ)	شَوَارِعُ	شَوَارِعُ	شَوَارِعُ	شَوَارِعُ	شَوَارِعُ

Sentence

اِتَّبِعْ الشَّارِعُ الرَّئِيسِي لِلْوُصُوْلِ إِلَى وِجْهَتُكَ

Follow the main road to get to your destination

Write your own sentence below!

44

عِقَارُ
Property/
Real Estate

Singular (مُفْرَد)	عِقَارُ	عِقَارُ	عِقَارُ	عِقَارُ
Plural (جَمْع)	عِقَارَاتُ	عِقَارَاتُ	عِقَارَاتُ	عِقَارَاتُ

Sentence

يَجِبُ عَلَيكَ أَنْ تَسْتَثْمِرَ فِي العِقَارَاتِ

You should invest in Property/Real Estate

Write your own sentence below!

شَرِكَةٌ
Company

Singular (مُفْرَدٌ)	شَرِكَةٌ	شَرِكَةٌ	شَرِكَةٌ	شَرِكَةٌ	شَرِكَةٌ
Plural (جَمْعٌ)	شَرِكَاتٌ	شَرِكَاتٌ	شَرِكَاتٌ	شَرِكَاتٌ	شَرِكَاتٌ

Sentence

هَذِهِ شَرِكَةٌ أَخْلَاقِيَّةٌ

This is an ethical company

Write your own sentence below!

46

دُكَّانٌ
Shop

| Singular (مُفْرَدٌ) | دُكَّانٌ | دُكَّانٌ | دُكَّانٌ | دُكَّانٌ |
| Plural (جَمْعٌ) | دَكَاكِينُ | دَكَاكِينُ | دَكَاكِينُ | دَكَاكِينُ |

Sentence

أُخْتِي زَارَتْ دُكَّانَ الأَحْذِيَةِ بِالأَمْسِ

My sister visited the shoe shop yesterday

Write your own sentence below!

48

مَقْهَى
Café

Singular (مُفْرَدٌ)	مَقْهَى	مَقْهَى	مَقْهَى	مَقْهَى
Plural (جَمْعٌ)	مَقْهَاةٌ	مَقْهَاةٌ	مَقْهَاةٌ	مَقْهَاةٌ

Sentence

هَلْ تَتَنَاوَلُ الفَطُورَ فِي المَنْزِلِ أَوْ تَذْهَبُ إِلَى المَقْهَى؟

Do you get breakfast at home, or go to the coffee shop?

Write your own sentence below!

مَطْعَمٌ
Restaurant

Singular (مُفْرَدٌ)	مَطْعَمٌ	مَطْعَمٌ	مَطْعَمٌ	مَطْعَمٌ
Plural (جَمْعٌ)	مَطَاعِمُ	مَطَاعِمُ	مَطَاعِمُ	مَطَاعِمُ

Sentence

كَمْ مَرَّةً تَأْكُلُ فِي الْمَطْعَمِ؟

How often do you eat out at a restaurant?

Write your own sentence below!

مَدْرَسَةٌ
School

Singular (مُفْرَدٌ)	مَدْرَسَةٌ	مَدْرَسَةٌ	مَدْرَسَةٌ	مَدْرَسَةٌ	مَدْرَسَةٌ
Plural (جَمْعٌ)	مَدَارِسُ	مَدَارِسُ	مَدَارِسُ	مَدَارِسُ	مَدَارِسُ

Sentence

مَا هُوَ شَكْلُ حُضُورِكَ فِي المَدْرَسَةِ؟

What's your school attendance like?

Write your own sentence below!

جَامِعَةٌ
University

Singular (مُفْرَدٌ)	جَامِعَةٌ	جَامِعَةٌ	جَامِعَةٌ	جَامِعَةٌ	
Plural (جَمْعٌ)	جَامِعَاتٌ	جَامِعَاتٌ	جَامِعَاتٌ	جَامِعَاتٌ	

Sentence

سَأَتَخَرَّجُ مِنْ الجَامِعَةِ هَذَا العَام

I will graduate from university this year

Write your own sentence below!

سِيَاحَةٌ
Tourism

| Singular (مُفْرَدٌ) | سِيَاحَةٌ | سِيَاحَةٌ | سِيَاحَةٌ | سِيَاحَةٌ |

Sentence

مَا هِيَ مَدِيْنَتُكَ الْمُفَضَّلَةِ لِلْسِيَاحَةِ؟

What is your favorite city for tourism

Write your own sentence below!

مَسْجِدٌ
Mosque

Singular (مُفرَدٌ)	مَسْجِدٌ	مَسْجِدٌ مَسْجِدٌ	مَسْجِدٌ	مَسْجِدٌ
Plural (جَمْعٌ)	مَسَاجِدُ	مَسَاجِدُ مَسَاجِدُ	مَسَاجِدُ	مَسَاجِدُ

Sentence

فِي أَيِّ مَسْجِدٍ تُصَلِّي؟

Which Mosque do you pray in?

Write your own sentence below!

كَنِيسَةٌ
Church

Singular (مُفْرَدٌ)	كَنِيسَةٌ	كَنِيسَةٌ	كَنِيسَةٌ	كَنِيسَةٌ	كَنِيسَةٌ
Plural (جَمْعٌ)	كَنَائِسُ	كَنَائِسُ	كَنَائِسُ	كَنَائِسُ	كَنَائِسُ

Sentence

هَذِهِ أَكْبَرُ كَنِيسَةٍ فِي أُورُوبَا

This is the biggest Church in Europe

Write your own sentence below!

فُنْدُقٌ
Hotel

Singular (مُفْرَد)	فُنْدُقٌ	فُنْدُقٌ	فُنْدُقٌ	فُنْدُقٌ
Plural (جَمْع)	فَنَادِقُ	فَنَادِقُ	فَنَادِقُ	فَنَادِقُ

Sentence

سَنَقْضِي اللَيْلَ فِي الفُنْدُقِ

We will spend the night at the hotel

Write your own sentence below!

مَطَارٌ
Airport

Singular (مُفْرَدٌ)	مَطَارٌ	مَطَارٌ	مَطَارٌ	مَطَارٌ	مَطَارٌ
Plural (جَمْعٌ)	مَطَارَاتٌ	مَطَارَاتٌ	مَطَارَاتٌ	مَطَارَاتٌ	مَطَارَاتٌ

Sentence

فِي أَيِّ مَطَارٍ سَتَهْبِطُ لَاحِقًا؟

At which airport will you land later?

Write your own sentence below!

مَتْحَفٌ

Museum

Singular (مُفرَدٌ)	مَتْحَفٌ	مَتْحَفٌ	مَتْحَفٌ	مَتْحَفٌ
Plural (جَمْعٌ)	مَتَاحِفُ	مَتَاحِفُ	مَتَاحِفُ	مَتَاحِفُ

Sentence

هَلْ زُرْتَ المَتْحَفَ الكَبِيرَ؟

Have you visited the grand museum?

Write your own sentence below!

مَصْرِفٌ / بَنْكٌ
Bank

Singular (مُفْرَدٌ)	مَصْرِفٌ, بَنْكٌ	مَصْرِفٌ, بَنْكٌ	مَصْرِفٌ, بَنْكٌ	مَصْرِفٌ, بَنْكٌ
Plural (جَمْعٌ)	مَصَارِفٌ, بُنُوكٌ	مَصَارِفٌ, بُنُوكٌ	مَصَارِفٌ, بُنُوكٌ	مَصَارِفٌ, بُنُوكٌ

Sentence

كَمْ مِنَ المَالِ لَدَيْكَ فِي البَنْكِ؟

How much money do you have in the bank?

Write your own sentence below!

58

مَكْتَبَةٌ
Library

Singular (مُفرَدٌ)	مَكْتَبَةٌ	مَكْتَبَةٌ	مَكْتَبَةٌ	مَكْتَبَةٌ
Plural (جَمْعٌ)	مَكْتَبَاتٌ	مَكْتَبَاتٌ	مَكْتَبَاتٌ	مَكْتَبَاتٌ

Sentence

يَجِبُ عَلَيْكَ القِيَامُ بِبَعْضِ الدِّرَاسَةِ الصَّامِتَةِ فِي المَكْتَبَةِ

You should do some silent study in the library

Write your own sentence below!

مُسْتَشْفَى
Hospital

| Singular (مُفْرَد) | مُسْتَشْفَى | مُسْتَشْفَى | مُسْتَشْفَى | مُسْتَشْفَى |
| Plural (جَمْع) | مُسْتَشْفَيَاتٌ | مُسْتَشْفَيَاتٌ | مُسْتَشْفَيَاتٌ | مُسْتَشْفَيَاتٌ |

Sentence

كُنْتُ فِي الْمُسْتَشْفَى آنِفًا بِسَبَبِ إِرْتِجَاجٍ فِي الْمُخِّ

I was in hospital earlier because of a concussion

Write your own sentence below!

عِيَادَةٌ
Clinic

Singular (مُفْرَدٌ)	عِيَادَةٌ	عِيَادَةٌ	عِيَادَةٌ	عِيَادَةٌ
Plural (جَمْعٌ)	عِيَادَاتٌ	عِيَادَاتٌ	عِيَادَاتٌ	عِيَادَاتٌ

Sentence

اِسْتَقْبَلْتُ مُوَظَّفَ الِاسْتِقْبَالِ فِي العِيَادَةِ بِابْتِسَامَةٍ

I greeted the receptionist at the clinic with a smile

Write your own sentence below!

61

صَيْدَلِيَّةٌ
Pharmacy

Singular (مُفْرَدٌ)	صَيْدَلِيَّةٌ	صَيْدَلِيَّةٌ	صَيْدَلِيَّةٌ	صَيْدَلِيَّةٌ	صَيْدَلِيَّةٌ
Plural (جَمْعٌ)	صَيْدَلِيَّاتٌ	صَيْدَلِيَّاتٌ	صَيْدَلِيَّاتٌ	صَيْدَلِيَّاتٌ	صَيْدَلِيَّاتٌ

Sentence

هَلْ حَصَلْتَ عَلَى دَوَائِكَ مِنْ الصَّيْدَلِيَّةِ؟

Did you get your medication from the pharmacy?

Write your own sentence below!

62

تَلَوُّثٌ
Pollution

Singular (مُفْرَدٌ)	تَلَوُّثٌ			

Sentence

التَّلَوُّثُ يُدَمِّرُ كُوْكَبَنا

Pollution is ruining our planet

Write your own sentence below!

63

مُوَاصَلَاتٌ

Public transport

Singular (مُفْرَدٌ)	مُوَاصَلَاتٌ	مُوَاصَلَاتٌ	مُوَاصَلَاتٌ	مُوَاصَلَاتٌ

Sentence

هَلْ تَأْخُذُ الْمُوَاصَلَاتِ الْعَامَّةَ إِلَى الْمَدْرَسَةِ أَمْ تَمْشِي عَلَى الْأَقْدَامِ؟

Do you take public transport to school or walk?

Write your own sentence below!

64

سَيَّارَةٌ
Car

Singular (مُفْرَدٌ)	سَيَّارَةٌ	سَيَّارَةٌ	سَيَّارَةٌ	سَيَّارَةٌ
Plural (جَمْعٌ)	سَيَّارَاتٌ	سَيَّارَاتٌ	سَيَّارَاتٌ	سَيَّارَاتٌ

Sentence

هَلْ سَيَّارَتُكَ بِنْزِينٌ اَمْ دِيزِلٌ؟

Is your car a petrol or diesel?

Write your own sentence below!

حَافِلَةٌ
Bus

Singular (مُفْرَد)	حَافِلَةٌ	حَافِلَةٌ	حَافِلَةٌ	حَافِلَةٌ
Plural (جَمْع)	حَوَافِلُ	حَوَافِلُ	حَوَافِلُ	حَوَافِلُ

Sentence

الحَافِلَةُ مُزْدَحِمَةٌ لِلْغَايَةِ فِي الصَّباح

The bus is very crowded in the mornings

Write your own sentence below!

دَرَّاجَةٌ
Bicycle

| Singular (مُفْرَدٌ) | دَرَّاجَةٌ | دَرَّاجَةٌ | دَرَّاجَةٌ | دَرَّاجَةٌ |
| Plural (جَمْعٌ) | دَرَّاجَاتٌ | دَرَّاجَاتٌ | دَرَّاجَاتٌ | دَرَّاجَاتٌ |

Sentence

سَقَطْتُ مِنْ دَرَّاجَتِي عِنْدَمَا كُنْتُ طِفْلاً

I fell of my bike as a kid

Write your own sentence below!

شَاحِنَةٌ
Lorry/Truck

Singular (مُفْرَدٌ)	**شَاحِنَةٌ**	شَاحِنَةٌ	شَاحِنَةٌ	شَاحِنَةٌ	شَاحِنَةٌ
Plural (جَمْعٌ)	**شَاحِنَاتٌ**	شَاحِنَاتٌ	شَاحِنَاتٌ	شَاحِنَاتٌ	شَاحِنَاتٌ

Sentence

تَمُرُّ الشَّاحِنَةُ بِمَنْزِلِي كُلَّ يَوْمٍ

The lorry drives past my house everyday

Write your own sentence below!

حَادِثَةٌ
Accident

Singular (مُفْرَدٌ)	حَادِثَةٌ	حَادِثَةٌ	حَادِثَةٌ	حَادِثَةٌ
Plural (جَمْعٌ)	حَوَادِثُ	حَوَادِثُ	حَوَادِثُ	حَوَادِثُ

Sentence

كَانَ هُنَاكَ حَادِثٌ كَبِيرٌ عَلَى الطَّرِيقِ السَّرِيعِ بِالْأَمْسِ

There was a big accident on the motorway yesterday

Write your own sentence below!

69

قِطَارٌ
Train

Singular (مُفْرَدٌ)	قِطَارٌ	قِطَارٌ	قِطَارٌ	قِطَارٌ
Plural (جَمْعٌ)	قِطَارَاتٌ	قِطَارَاتٌ	قِطَارَاتٌ	قِطَارَاتٌ

Sentence

أُسَافِرُ كَثِيراً بِالْقِطَارِ

I travel a lot by train

Write your own sentence below!

مَرْكَبٌ
Boat

| Singular (مُفْرَدٌ) | مَرْكَبٌ | مَرْكَبٌ | مَرْكَبٌ | مَرْكَبٌ |
| Plural (جَمْعٌ) | مَرَاكِبُ | مَرَاكِبُ | مَرَاكِبُ | مَرَاكِبُ |

Sentence

غَرِقَ المَرْكَبُ فِي البَحْرِ

The boat Sunk in the sea

Write your own sentence below!

سَفِينَةٌ
Ship

Singular (مُفْرَد)	سَفِينَةٌ	سَفِينَةٌ	سَفِينَةٌ	سَفِينَةٌ
Plural (جَمْعٌ)	سُفُنٌ	سُفُنٌ	سُفُنٌ	سُفُنٌ

Sentence

السَّفِينَةُ كَانَ بِدَاخِلِهَا أَلْفَ شَخْصٍ

The ship had a thousand people inside

Write your own sentence below!

طَائِرَةٌ
Plane

Singular (مُفْرَد)	طَائِرَةٌ	طَائِرَةٌ	طَائِرَةٌ	طَائِرَةٌ	طَائِرَةٌ
Plural (جَمْع)	طَائِرَاتٌ	طَائِرَاتٌ	طَائِرَاتٌ	طَائِرَاتٌ	طَائِرَاتٌ

Sentence

أَشْعُرُ بِالْقَلِقِ عِنْدَمَا أُسَافِرُ بِالْطَّائِرَةِ

I feel anxious when travelling by plane

Write your own sentence below!

جَوْلَةٌ
Tour

Singular (مُفْرَدٌ)	جَوْلَةٌ	جَوْلَةٌ	جَوْلَةٌ	جَوْلَةٌ
Plural (جَمْعٌ)	جَوْلَاتٌ	جَوْلَاتٌ	جَوْلَاتٌ	جَوْلَاتٌ

Sentence

هَلْ تُفَضِّلُ جَوْلَةً جَمَاعِيَّةً أَمْ السَّفَرَ بِفَرْدِكَ؟

Do you prefer a group tour, or travelling alone?

Write your own sentence below!

مَلْبَسٌ
Clothes

Singular (مُفْرَدٌ)	مَلْبَسٌ	مَلْبَسٌ	مَلْبَسٌ	مَلْبَسٌ
Plural (جَمْعٌ)	مَلَابِسٌ	مَلَابِسٌ	مَلَابِسٌ	مَلَابِسٌ

Sentence

أَنَا أُحِبُّ أُسْلُوْبَكَ فِي الْمَلَابِسِ

I like your style of clothing

Write your own sentence below!

أَنِيقٌ
Elegant/Stylish

| Singular (مُفْرَد) | أَنِيقٌ | | | | |

Sentence

بَدْلَةُ زِفَافِكَ أَنِيقَةٌ يَا عَبَّاس

Your wedding suit is very elegant, Abbas

Write your own sentence below!

قَمِيصٌ
Shirt

Singular (مُفْرَدٌ)	قَمِيصٌ	قَمِيصٌ	قَمِيصٌ	قَمِيصٌ
Plural (جَمْعٌ)	قُمْصَانٌ	قُمْصَانٌ	قُمْصَانٌ	قُمْصَانٌ

Sentence

أَغْسِلُ قُمْصَانَ المَدْرَسَةِ كُلَّ يَوْمِ جُمْعَةٍ

I wash my school shirts every Friday

Write your own sentence below!

مِعْطَفٌ
Coat

| Singular (مُفْرَدٌ) | مِعْطَفٌ | مِعْطَفٌ | مِعْطَفٌ | مِعْطَفٌ |
| Plural (جَمْعٌ) | مَعَاطِفُ | مَعَاطِفُ | مَعَاطِفُ | مَعَاطِفُ |

Sentence

مِنْ أَيْنَ اِشْتَرَيْتَ مِعْطَفَكَ؟ هُوَ جَمِيلٌ

Where did you buy your jacket from? It's beautiful

Write your own sentence below!

فُسْتَانٌ
Dress

Singular (مُفْرَدٌ)	فُسْتَانٌ	فُسْتَانٌ	فُسْتَانٌ	فُسْتَانٌ	فُسْتَانٌ
Plural (جَمْعٌ)	فَسَاتِينُ	فَسَاتِينُ	فَسَاتِينُ	فَسَاتِينُ	فَسَاتِينُ

Sentence

لَا أُحِبُّ اِرْتِدَاءَ فُسْتَانِي لِأَنَّهَا غَيْرُ مَرِيْحَةٍ

I don't like wearing my dress because it is uncomfortable

Write your own sentence below!

قُبَعَةٌ
Hat

Singular (مُفْرَد)	قُبَعَةٌ	قُبَعَةٌ	قُبَعَةٌ	قُبَعَةٌ
Plural (جَمْع)	قُبَعَاتٌ	قُبَعَاتٌ	قُبَعَاتٌ	قُبَعَاتٌ

Sentence

اِرْتَدَيْتُ قُبَعَتِي لِتَحْمِينِي مِنْ الشَّمْسِ

I wore my hat so it could protect me from the sun

Write your own sentence below!

قُفَّازٌ
Gloves

Singular (مُفْرَدٌ)	قُفَّازٌ	قُفَّازٌ	قُفَّازٌ	قُفَّازٌ
Plural (جَمْعٌ)	قُفَّازَاتٌ	قُفَّازَاتٌ	قُفَّازَاتٌ	قُفَّازَاتٌ

Sentence

لاَ أَسْتَطِيعُ الْخُرُوجَ فِي الشِّتَاءِ بِدُونِ قُفَّازِي

I can't go out in the winter without my gloves

Write your own sentence below!

حِزَامٌ
Belt

Singular (مُفْرَدٌ)	حِزَامٌ	حِزَامٌ	حِزَامٌ	حِزَامٌ
Plural (جَمْعٌ)	أَحْزِمَةٌ	أَحْزِمَةٌ	أَحْزِمَةٌ	أَحْزِمَةٌ

Sentence

أُحِبُّ أَنْ أَلْبَسَ حِزَامِي ضَيِّقٌ

I like to wear my belt tight

Write your own sentence below!

جَوْرَبٌ
Socks

Singular (مُفْرَدٌ)	جَوْرَبٌ	جَوْرَبٌ	جَوْرَبٌ	جَوْرَبٌ
Plural (جَمْعٌ)	جَوَارِبُ	جَوَارِبُ	جَوَارِبُ	جَوَارِبُ

Sentence

هَلْ تَتَطَابَقُ جَوَارِبُكَ مَعَ مَلَابِسِكَ اليَوْمَ؟

Are you matching your socks with your outfit today?

Write your own sentence below!

حِذَاءٌ
Shoes

Singular (مُفْرَدٌ)	حِذَاءٌ	حِذَاءٌ	حِذَاءٌ	حِذَاءٌ
Plural (جَمْعٌ)	أَحْذِيَةٌ	أَحْذِيَةٌ	أَحْذِيَةٌ	أَحْذِيَةٌ

Sentence

نَسِيتُ حِذَائِي لِفَصْلِ الرِّيَاضَةِ

I forgot my shoes for sports class

Write your own sentence below!

جَوْهَرَةٌ
Jewelry

Singular (مُفْرَد)	جَوْهَرَةٌ	جَوْهَرَةٌ	جَوْهَرَةٌ	جَوْهَرَةٌ
Plural (جَمْع)	جَوَاهِرُ/جَوْهَرَاتٌ	جَوَاهِرُ	جَوَاهِرُ	جَوَاهِرُ

Sentence

زَوْجَتِي تُحِبُّ المُجَوْهَرَاتِ

My wife loves jewelry

Write your own sentence below!

قِلَادَةٌ
Necklace

Singular (مُفْرَدٌ)	قِلَادَةٌ	قِلَادَةٌ	قِلَادَةٌ	قِلَادَةٌ	
Plural (جَمْعٌ)	قَلَائِدُ	قَلَائِدُ	قَلَائِدُ	قَلَائِدُ	

Sentence

كَانَ لَدَى صَدِيقَتِي قِلَادَةٌ جَمِيلَةٌ فِي يَوْمِ زِفَافِهَا

My friend had a beautiful necklace on her wedding day

Write your own sentence below!

ذَهَبٌ
Gold

Singular (مُفْرَدٌ)	ذَهَبٌ	ذَهَبٌ	ذَهَبٌ	ذَهَبٌ

Sentence

الذَهَبُ اِسْتِثْمَارٌ ذَكِيٌّ

Gold is a smart investment

Write your own sentence below!

فِضَّةٌ
Silver

Singular (مُفْرَد)	فِضَّةٌ	فِضَّةٌ	فِضَّةٌ	فِضَّةٌ

Sentence

الفِضَّةُ لَا تَصْدَأُ أَوْ تَتَآكَلُ

Silver does not rust or corrode

Write your own sentence below!

نَظَّارَةٌ
Glasses

Singular (مُفْرَدٌ)	نَظَّارَةٌ	نَظَّارَة	نَظَّارَة	نَظَّارَة
Plural (جَمْعٌ)	نَظَّارَاتٌ	نَظَّارَاتٌ	نَظَّارَاتٌ	نَظَّارَاتٌ

Sentence

لَا أَسْتَطِيعُ القِرَاءةَ بِدُوْنِ نَظَّارَتِي

I can't read without my glasses

Write your own sentence below!

شَنْطَةٌ
Suitcase

Singular (مُفْرَد)	شَنْطَةٌ	شَنْطَةٌ	شَنْطَةٌ	شَنْطَةٌ
Plural (جَمْع)	شِنَطٌ	شِنَطٌ	شِنَطٌ	شِنَطٌ

Sentence

أُسَافِرُ مَعَ شَنْطَةِ سَفَرٍ خَفِيفَةٍ

I travel with a light suitcase

Write your own sentence below!

مِظَلَّةٌ
Umbrella

Singular (مُفْرَد)	مِظَلَّةٌ	مِظَلَّةٌ	مِظَلَّةٌ	مِظَلَّةٌ
Plural (جَمْع)	مِظَلَّاتٌ	مِظَلَّاتٌ	مِظَلَّاتٌ	مِظَلَّاتٌ

Sentence

أَحْمِلُ دَائِمًا مِظَلَّةً فِي حَالَةِ تَغَيُّرِ الجَوِّ

I always carry an umbrella incase the weather changes

Write your own sentence below!

Singular (مُفْرَد)	حَضَانَةٌ	حَضَانَةٌ	حَضَانَةٌ	حَضَانَةٌ	حَضَانَةٌ
Plural (جَمْعٌ)	حَضَانَاتٌ	حَضَانَاتٌ	حَضَانَاتٌ	حَضَانَاتٌ	حَضَانَاتٌ

Sentence

لَدَيَّ بَعْضُ الذِكْرِيَاتِ مِنْ الحَضَانَةِ

I have some good memories from nursery

Write your own sentence below!

المَدْرَسَةُ الاِبْتِدَائِيَّةُ
Elementary School

| Singular (مُفْرَدٌ) | المَدْرَسَةُ الاِبْتِدَائِيَّةُ | المَدْرَسَةُ الاِبْتِدَائِيَّةُ | المَدْرَسَةُ الاِبْتِدَائِيَّةُ | المَدْرَسَةُ الاِبْتِدَائِيَّةُ |

Sentence

كُنْتُ مَشْهُورًا جِدًّا فِي المَدْرَسَةِ الاِبْتِدَائِيَّةِ

I was very popular at elementary school

Write your own sentence below!

المَدْرَسَةُ الثَّانَوِيَّةُ
Secondary School

	المَدْرَسَةُ الثَّانَوِيَّةُ	المَدْرَسَةُ الثَّانَوِيَّةُ	المَدْرَسَةُ الثَّانَوِيَّةُ	المَدْرَسَةُ الثَّانَوِيَّةُ
ular (مُفْرَد)				

Sentence

نَجَحْتُ فِي اِمْتِحَانَاتِي فِي المَدْرَسَةِ الثَّانَوِيَّةِ

I passed my exams in secondary school

Write your own sentence below!

مَعْهَدُ
Faculty

Singular (مُفْرَدٌ)	مَعْهَدُ	مَعْهَدُ	مَعْهَدُ	مَعْهَدُ
Plural (جَمْعٌ)	مَعَاهِدُ	مَعَاهِدُ	مَعَاهِدُ	مَعَاهِدُ

Sentence

فِي أَيِّ مَعْهَدٍ تَدْرُسُ؟

Which faculty do you study in?

Write your own sentence below!

بَرْنَامِجٌ
Program

| Singular (مُفْرَدٌ) | بَرْنَامِجٌ | بَرْنَامِجٌ | بَرْنَامِجٌ | بَرْنَامِجٌ |
| Plural (جَمْعٌ) | بَرَامِجُ | بَرَامِجُ | بَرَامِجُ | بَرَامِجُ |

Sentence

هَلْ قُمْتَ بِالتَّسْجِيلِ فِي بَرْنَامِجِ الرِّيَاضِيَّاتِ؟

Did you sign up for the maths program?

Write your own sentence below!

مَادَّةٌ
Subject

| Singular (مُفْرَدٌ) | مَادَّةٌ | مَادَّةٌ | مَادَّةٌ | مَادَّةٌ |
| Plural (جَمْعٌ) | مَوَادُّ | مَوَادُّ | مَوَادُّ | مَوَادُّ |

Sentence

مَاذَا كَانَتْ مَادَّتُكَ الدِّرَاسِيَةِ المُفَضَّلَةِ فِي المَدْرَسَةِ؟

What was your favorite subject in school?

Write your own sentence below!

شَهَادَةٌ
Certificate

Singular (مُفْرَدٌ)	شَهَادَةٌ	شَهَادَةٌ	شَهَادَةٌ	شَهَادَةٌ
Plural (جَمْعٌ)	شَهَادَاتٌ	شَهَادَاتٌ	شَهَادَاتٌ	شَهَادَاتٌ

Sentence

هَلْ حَصَلْتَ عَلَى شَهَادَتِكَ الجَامَعِيَةِ عَبْرَ البَرِيدِ بَعْدُ؟

Have you received your university certificate through the post yet?

Write your own sentence below!

مُدَرِّسٌ
Teacher

Singular (مُفْرَدٌ)	مُدَرِّسٌ	مُدَرِّس	مُدَرِّس	مُدَرِّس
Plural (جَمْعٌ)	مُدَرِّسُوْنَ	مُدَرِّسُوْنَ	مُدَرِّسُوْنَ	مُدَرِّسُوْنَ

Sentence

أَطْمَحُ لِأَنْ أَصْبَحَ مُدَرِّسًا عِنْدَمَا أَكْبَرُ

I aspire to be a teacher when I am older

Write your own sentence below!

طَالِبٌ
Student

Singular (مُفْرَدٌ)	طَالِبٌ	طَالِبٌ	طَالِبٌ	طَالِبٌ	طَالِبٌ
Plural (جَمْعٌ)	طُلَّابٌ	طُلَّابٌ	طُلَّابٌ	طُلَّابٌ	طُلَّابٌ

Sentence

أَنَا أَفْضَلُ طَالِبٍ فِي صَفِّي

I am the best student in my class

Write your own sentence below!

وَاجِبٌ
Homework

Singular (مُفْرَدٌ)	وَاجِبٌ	وَاجِبٌ	وَاجِبٌ	وَاجِبٌ	وَاجِبٌ
Plural (جَمْعٌ)	وَاجِبَاتٌ	وَاجِبَاتٌ	وَاجِبَاتٌ	وَاجِبَاتٌ	وَاجِبَاتٌ

Sentence

لاَ تَتْرُكْ وَاجِبَكَ إِلَى اللَّحْظَةِ الأَخِيرَةِ!

Don't leave your homework until the last minute!

Write your own sentence below!

اِمْتِحَانٌ
Test

Singular (مُفْرَدٌ)	اِمْتِحَانٌ اِمْتِحَانٌ اِمْتِحَانٌ اِمْتِحَانٌ **اِمْتِحَانٌ**
Plural (جَمْعٌ)	اِمْتِحَانَاتٌ اِمْتِحَانَاتٌ اِمْتِحَانَاتٌ اِمْتِحَانَاتٌ **اِمْتِحَانَاتٌ**

Sentence

نَجَحْتُ فِي اِمْتِحَانَاتِي بِنَجَاحٍ بَاهِرٍ

I passed my exams with flying colors

Write your own sentence below!

مُحَاضَرَةٌ
Lecture

Singular (مُفْرَدٌ)	مُحَاضَرَةٌ	مُحَاضَرَةٌ	مُحَاضَرَةٌ	مُحَاضَرَةٌ
Plural (جَمْعٌ)	مُحَاضَرَاتٌ	مُحَاضَرَاتٌ	مُحَاضَرَاتٌ	مُحَاضَرَاتٌ

Sentence

لَمْ أَحْضَرِ المُحَاضَرَةُ بِسَبَبِ مَرَضِي

I didn't attend the lecture because of my illness

Write your own sentence below!

مُنَاقَشَةٌ
Discussion

Singular (مُفْرَدٌ)	مُنَاقَشَةٌ	مُنَاقَشَةٌ	مُنَاقَشَةٌ	مُنَاقَشَةٌ
Plural (جَمْعٌ)	مُنَاقَشَاتٌ	مُنَاقَشَاتٌ	مُنَاقَشَاتٌ	مُنَاقَشَاتٌ

Sentence

اِنْضَمَمْتُ إِلَى الْمُنَاقَشَةِ السَّاخِنَةِ بَيْنَ الطُّلَابِ

I joined the heated discussion between the students

Write your own sentence below!

دَفْتَرٌ
Notebook

Singular (مُفْرَدٌ)	دَفْتَرٌ	دَفْتَرٌ	دَفْتَرٌ	دَفْتَرٌ
Plural (جَمْعٌ)	دَفَاتِرُ	دَفَاتِرُ	دَفَاتِرُ	دَفَاتِرُ

Sentence

اِسْتَخْدَمْتُ دَفْتَرَ مُلَاحَظَاتِي لِلْمُرَاجَعَةِ مِنْ أَجْلِ الِامْتِحَانِ

I used my notebook to revise for the exam

Write your own sentence below!

قَلَمٌ
Pen

| Singular (مُفْرَدٌ) | قَلَمٌ | قَلَمٌ | قَلَمٌ | قَلَمٌ |
| Plural (جَمْعٌ) | أَقْلَامٌ | أَقْلَامٌ | أَقْلَامٌ | أَقْلَامٌ |

Sentence

لَدَيَّ قَلَمٌ اِحْتِيَاطِيٌّ فِي حَالَةِ نَفَادِ الحِبْرِ

I have a reserve pen in case I run out of ink

Write your own sentence below!

وَرَقَةٌ
Paper

| Singular (مُفْرَدٌ) | وَرَقَةٌ | وَرَقَةٌ | وَرَقَةٌ | وَرَقَةٌ |
| Plural (جَمْعٌ) | أَوْرَاقٌ | أَوْرَاقٌ | أَوْرَاقٌ | أَوْرَاقٌ |

Sentence

لَا تُضَيِّعْ الْوَرَقَ فِي الطَّابِعَةِ

Don't waste paper in the printer

Write your own sentence below!

مِمْحَاةٌ
Eraser

Singular (مُفْرَدٌ)	**مِمْحَاةٌ**	مِمْحَاةٌ	مِمْحَاةٌ	مِمْحَاةٌ
Plural (جَمْعٌ)	**مِمْحَاوَاتٌ**	مِمْحَاوَاتٌ	مِمْحَاوَاتٌ	مِمْحَاوَاتٌ

Sentence

فَقَدْتُ مِمْحَاتِي فِي المَدْرَسَةِ

I lost my eraser in school

Write your own sentence below!

سَبُّورَةٌ
Blackboard

Singular (مُفْرَدٌ)	سَبُّورَةٌ	سَبُّورَةٌ	سَبُّورَةٌ	سَبُّورَةٌ
Plural (جَمْعٌ)	سَبُّورَاتٌ	سَبُّورَاتٌ	سَبُّورَاتٌ	سَبُّورَاتٌ

Sentence

أَتَعَلَّمُ بِشَكْلٍ أَفْضَلٍ مَعَ السَّبُّورَةِ

I learn better with a blackboard

Write your own sentence below!

مِسْطَرَةٌ
Ruler

Singular (مُفْرَدٌ)	مِسْطَرَةٌ	مِسْطَرَةٌ	مِسْطَرَةٌ	مِسْطَرَةٌ
Plural (جَمْعٌ)	مَسَاطِرُ	مَسَاطِرُ	مَسَاطِرُ	مَسَاطِرُ

Sentence

الْمِسْطَرَةُ إِلْزَامِيَّةٌ لِفَصْلِ الرِّيَاضِيَّاتِ

A ruler is mandatory for maths class

Write your own sentence below!

مُعْجَمٌ
Dictionary

Singular (مُفْرَدٌ)	مُعْجَمٌ	مُعْجَمٌ	مُعْجَمٌ	مُعْجَمٌ
Plural (جَمْعٌ)	مَعَاجِمُ	مَعَاجِمُ	مَعَاجِمُ	مَعَاجِمُ

Sentence

اللُّغَةُ الْعَرَبِيَّةُ لَدَيْهَا وَاحِدَةٌ مِنْ أَكْبَرِ الْمَعَاجِمِ

Arabic has one of the largest dictionaries

Write your own sentence below!

مَهَارَةٌ
Skills

Singular (مُفْرَدٌ)	مَهَارَةٌ	مَهَارَةٌ	مَهَارَةٌ	مَهَارَةٌ	مَهَارَةٌ
Plural (جَمْعٌ)	مَهَارَاتٌ	مَهَارَاتٌ	مَهَارَاتٌ	مَهَارَاتٌ	مَهَارَاتٌ

Sentence

أَنَا مَاهِرٌ جِدًّا فِي الْجُغْرَافِيَا

I am very skilled at geography

Write your own sentence below!

Singular (مُفْرَدٌ)	هِوَايَةٌ	هِوَايَةٌ	هِوَايَةٌ	هِوَايَةٌ
Plural (جَمْعٌ)	هِوَايَاتٌ	هِوَايَاتٌ	هِوَايَاتٌ	هِوَايَاتٌ

Sentence

كَمْ عَدَدُ الهِوَايَاتِ لَدَيْكَ؟

How many hobbies do you have?

Write your own sentence below!

كُرَةُ الْقَدَمِ
Soccer/Football

Singular (مُفْرَدٌ)	كُرَةُ الْقَدَمِ	كُرَةُ الْقَدَمِ	كُرَةُ الْقَدَمِ	كُرَةُ الْقَدَمِ

Sentence

أَيُّ فَرِيقِ كُرَةِ قَدَمٍ تَتَشَجَّعُ؟

Which football team do you support?

Write your own sentence below!

مَلْعَبُ
Field

Singular (مُفْرَدٌ)	مَلْعَبٌ	مَلْعَبٌ	مَلْعَبٌ	مَلْعَبٌ
Plural (جَمْعٌ)	مَلَاعِبُ	مَلَاعِبُ	مَلَاعِبُ	مَلَاعِبُ

Sentence

يُوجَدُ مَلْعَبٌ كَبِيرٌ بِالقُرْبِ مِنْ مَنْزِلِي

There is a big field near my house

Write your own sentence below!

مُدَرِّبٌ
Trainer/Coach

Singular (مُفْرَدٌ)	مُدَرِّبٌ	مُدَرِّبٌ	مُدَرِّبٌ	مُدَرِّبٌ
Plural (جَمْعٌ)	مُدَرِّبُونَ	مُدَرِّبُونَ	مُدَرِّبُونَ	مُدَرِّبُونَ

Sentence

هَلْ وَجَدْتَ مُدَرِّبًا جَدِيدًا لِلْمُسَابَقَةِ؟

Have you found a new coach for the competition?

Write your own sentence below!

مُحْتَرِفٌ
Professional

Singular (مُفْرَدٌ)	مُحْتَرِفٌ	مُحْتَرِفٌ	مُحْتَرِفٌ	مُحْتَرِفٌ
Plural (جَمْعٌ)	مُحْتَرِفُونَ	مُحْتَرِفُونَ	مُحْتَرِفُونَ	مُحْتَرِفُونَ

Sentence

يَتَدَرَّبُ الرِّيَاضِيُّونَ الْمُحْتَرِفُونَ بِجَدٍّ كُلَّ يَوْمٍ

Professional athletes train hard everyday

Write your own sentence below!

كُرَةُ السَّلَّةِ
Basketball

| Singular (مُفْرَد) | كُرَةُ السَّلَّةِ | كُرَةُ السَّلَّةِ | كُرَةُ السَّلَّةِ | كُرَةُ السَّلَّةِ |

Sentence

كُرَةُ السَّلَّةِ هِيَ رِيَاضَةٌ مُرْهِقَةٌ

Basketball is a tiring sport

Write your own sentence below!

118

كُرَةُ الطَّائِرَةِ
Volleyball

| Singular (مُفْرَد) | كُرَةُ الطَّائِرَة | كُرَةُ الطَّائِرَة | كُرَةُ الطَّائِرَة | كُرَةُ الطَّائِرَة | كُرَةُ الطَّائِرَة |

Sentence

لَعِبْتُ الكُرَةَ الطَّائِرَةِ بَعْدَ اِمْتِحَانِي

I played volleyball after my exam

Write your own sentence below!

سِبَاحَةٌ
Swimming

| Singular (مُفْرَد) | سِبَاحَةٌ | سِبَاحَةٌ | سِبَاحَةٌ | سِبَاحَةٌ |

Sentence

السِبَاحَةُ رَائِعَةٌ لِإرْخَاءِ عَضَلَاتِكَ

Swimming is great for relaxing your muscles

Write your own sentence below!

(120)

مُضْحِكٌ
Funny

| Singular (مُفْرَدٌ) | مُضْحِكٌ | مُضْحِكٌ | مُضْحِكٌ | مُضْحِكٌ |
| Plural (جَمْعٌ) | مُضْحِكُونَ | مُضْحِكُونَ | مُضْحِكُونَ | مُضْحِكُونَ |

Sentence

أُحِبُّ مُشَاهَدَةَ الْمُسَلْسَلَاتِ التَّلْفِزْيُونِيَّةَ الْمُضْحِكَةَ

I like to watch funny TV shows

Write your own sentence below!

مُتَفَائِلٌ
Optimistic

Singular (مُفْرَدٌ)	مُتَفَائِلٌ	مُتَفَائِلٌ	مُتَفَائِلٌ	مُتَفَائِلٌ
Plural (جَمْعٌ)	مُتَفَائِلُونَ	مُتَفَائِلُونَ	مُتَفَائِلُونَ	مُتَفَائِلُونَ

Sentence

أُحِبُّ أَنْ أَكُونَ مُتَفَائِلًا فِي أَوْقَاتِ الشِّدَّةِ

I like to be optimistic during times of hardship

Write your own sentence below!

مُتَشَائِمٌ
Pessimistic

Singular (مُفْرَدٌ)	مُتَشَائِمٌ	مُتَشَائِمٌ	مُتَشَائِمٌ	مُتَشَائِمٌ
Plural (جَمْعٌ)	مُتَشَائِمُونَ	مُتَشَائِمُونَ	مُتَشَائِمُونَ	مُتَشَائِمُونَ

Sentence

أَنَا لَا أَتَسَكَّعُ مَعَ الْمُتَشَائِمِينَ

I don't hang out with pessimistic people

Write your own sentence below!

قَاسٍ
Cruel

Singular (مُفْرَدٌ)	قَاسٍ	قَاسٍ	قَاسٍ	قَاسٍ
Plural (جَمْعٌ)	قَاسُوْنَ	قَاسُوْنَ	قَاسُوْنَ	قَاسُوْنَ

Sentence

لَا تَكُنْ قَاسِيًا مَعَ أَشْقَائِكَ

Don't be cruel with your siblings

Write your own sentence below!

صَادِقٌ
Truthful

| Singular (مُفْرَدٌ) | صَادِقٌ | صَادِقٌ | صَادِقٌ | صَادِقٌ |
| Plural (جَمْعٌ) | صَادِقُونَ | صَادِقُونَ | صَادِقُونَ | صَادِقُونَ |

Sentence

نَصَحَنِي وَالِدَيَّ أَنْ أَكُونَ دَائِمًا صَادِقًا

My parents advised me to always be truthful

Write your own sentence below!

شَاطِرٌ
Clever

Singular (مُفْرَد)	شَاطِرٌ	شَاطِرٌ	شَاطِرٌ	شَاطِرٌ	
Plural (جَمْع)	شَاطِرُونَ	شَاطِرُونَ	شَاطِرُونَ	شَاطِرُونَ	

Sentence

قَالَ لِي أُسْتَاذِي "أَنْتَ وَلَدٌ شَاطِرٌ لَقَدْ حَقَّقْتَ أَعْلَى دَرَجَةٍ فِي الفَصْلِ!"

My teacher told me "You clever boy! You achieved the highest grade in the class!"

Write your own sentence below!

غَبِيٌّ
Stupid/Foolish

| Singular (مُفْرَد) | غَبِيٌّ | غَبِيٌّ | غَبِيٌّ | غَبِيٌّ |
| Plural (جَمْع) | أَغْبِيَاء | أَغْبِيَاء | أَغْبِيَاء | أَغْبِيَاء |

Sentence

لَا تَسْتَمِعْ إلى الأَغْبِيَاءِ

Don't listen to foolish people

Write your own sentence below!

مَجْنُونٌ
Insane/Crazy

Singular (مُفْرَدٌ)	**مَجْنُونٌ**	مَجْنُونٌ	مَجْنُونٌ	مَجْنُونٌ
Plural (جَمْعٌ)	**مَجَانِينُ**	مَجَانِينُ	مَجَانِينُ	مَجَانِينُ

Sentence

هَلْ رَأَيْتَ الْجَرِيمَةَ الَّتِي اِرْتَكَبَهَا الْمَجْنُونُ فِي الْأَخْبَارِ؟

Did you see the crime committed by the crazy guy on the news?

Write your own sentence below!

مُتَوَاضِعٌ
Humble

Singular (مُفْرَدٌ)	مُتَوَاضِعٌ	مُتَوَاضِعٌ	مُتَوَاضِعٌ	مُتَوَاضِعٌ
Plural (جَمْعٌ)	مُتَوَاضِعُونَ	مُتَوَاضِعُونَ	مُتَوَاضِعُونَ	مُتَوَاضِعُونَ

Sentence

كُنْ مُتَوَاضِعًا دَائِمًا، بِغَضِّ النَّظَرِ عَنْ وَضْعِكَ فِي الْحَيَاةِ

Always be humble, no matter your status in life

Write your own sentence below!

جَبَانٌ
Coward

| Singular (مُفْرَدٌ) | جَبَانٌ | جَبَانٌ | جَبَانٌ | جَبَانٌ |
| Plural (جَمْعٌ) | جُبَنَاءُ | جُبَنَاءُ | جُبَنَاءُ | جُبَنَاءُ |

Sentence

ضَرَبَ الجُبَنَاءُ الصَّبِيَّ وَهَرَبُوا

The Cowards hit the boy and ran away

Write your own sentence below!

شُجَاعٌ
Brave

Singular (مُفْرَدٌ)	شُجَاعٌ	شُجَاعٌ	شُجَاعٌ	شُجَاعٌ
Plural (جَمْعٌ)	شُجَاعُونَ	شُجَاعُونَ	شُجَاعُونَ	شُجَاعُونَ

Sentence

قَامَ الصَّبِيُّ الشُّجَاعُ بِحِمَايَةِ أُخْتِهِ مِنَ الْمُتَنَمِّرِينَ عَلَيْهَا

The brave boy protected his sister from her bullies

Write your own sentence below!

كَسْلَانٌ
Lazy

Singular (مُفْرَدٌ)	كَسْلَانٌ	كَسْلَانٌ	كَسْلَانٌ	كَسْلَانٌ	كَسْلَانٌ
Plural (جَمْعٌ)	كَسَالَى	كَسَالَى	كَسَالَى	كَسَالَى	كَسَالَى

Sentence

لَا تَكُنْ كَسُوْلًا يَا عَبَّاس ، قُمْ بِالْأَعْمَالِ الْمَنْزِلِيَةِ!

Don't be lazy Abbas, do your chores!

Write your own sentence below!

مُؤَدَّبٌ
Polite

| Singular (مُفْرَدٌ) | مُؤَدَّبٌ | مُؤَدَّب | مُؤَدَّب | مُؤَدَّب |
| Plural (جَمْعٌ) | مُؤَدَّبُوْنَ | مُؤَدَّبُوْنَ | مُؤَدَّبُوْنَ | مُؤَدَّبُوْنَ |

Sentence

كَانَ الْمُعَلِّمُ مُؤَدَّبًا جِدًّا مَعَ وَالِدَيَّ اللَّيْلَةَ الْمَاضِيَةَ

The teacher was very polite to my parents last night

Write your own sentence below!

مُهْمِل
Careless/Negligent

Singular (مُفْرَدٌ)	مُهْمِل	مُهْمِل	مُهْمِل	مُهْمِل
Plural (جَمْعٌ)	مُهْمِلُوْنَ	مُهْمِلُوْنَ	مُهْمِلُوْنَ	مُهْمِلُوْنَ

Sentence

لِمَاذَا أَنْتَ مُهْمِلٌ جِدًّا فِي مُتَعَلَّقَاتِكَ يَا بُنَيَّ؟

Why are you so negligent over your belongings, son?

Write your own sentence below!

بَخِيلٌ
Stingy/Cheap

Singular (مُفْرَدٌ)	بَخِيلٌ	بَخِيلٌ	بَخِيلٌ	بَخِيلٌ
Plural (جَمْعٌ)	بُخَلَاءُ	بُخَلَاءُ	بُخَلَاءُ	بُخَلَاءُ

Sentence

كَانَتْ مَارِيَّا بَخِيلَةً مَعَ حَلْوِيَّاتِهَا، وَلَمْ تُشَارِكْهَا مَعَ أَصْدِقَائِهَا

Maria was stingy with her sweets, she did not share with her friends

Write your own sentence below!

كَرِيمٌ
Generous

Singular (مُفْرَدٌ)	كَرِيمٌ	كَرِيمٌ	كَرِيمٌ	كَرِيمٌ	كَرِيمٌ
Plural (جَمْعٌ)	كِرَامٌ	كِرَامٌ	كِرَامٌ	كِرَامٌ	كِرَامٌ

Sentence

كَوْنُكَ كَرِيمًا هُوَ مِنْ أَفْضَلِ السِّمَاتِ الَّتِي يُمْكِنُ أَنْ يَتَمَتَّعَ بِهَا الشَّخْصُ

Being generous is one of the best traits a person can have

Write your own sentence below!

عَنِيْدٌ
Stubborn

Singular (مُفْرَدٌ)	عَنِيْدٌ	عَنِيْد	عَنِيْد	عَنِيْد
Plural (جَمْعٌ)	عَنِيْدُوْنَ	عَنِيْدُوْنَ	عَنِيْدُوْن	عَنِيْدُوْن

Sentence

لَمْ يَأْخُذْ الصَّبِيُّ نَصِيْحَةَ آبَائِهِ لِإنَّهُ كَانَ عَنِيْداً

The boy did not take his father's advice because he was stubborn

Write your own sentence below!

نَعْسَانٌ
Tired/drowsy

Singular (مُفْرَدٌ)	نَعْسَانٌ	نَعْسَانٌ	نَعْسَانٌ	نَعْسَانٌ
Plural (جَمْعٌ)	نِعَاس	نِعَاس	نِعَاس	نِعَاس

Sentence

أَشْعُرُ بِالنِّعَاسِ بَعْدَ يَوْمٍ طَوِيلٍ فِي العَمَلِ

I feel tired after a long day at work

Write your own sentence below!

وَاثِقٌ
Confident

Singular (مُفْرَد)	وَاثِقٌ	وَاثِقٌ	وَاثِقٌ	وَاثِقٌ
Plural (جَمْع)	وَاثِقُوْنَ	وَاثِقُوْنَ	وَاثِقُوْنَ	وَاثِقُوْنَ

Sentence

يَجِبُ أَنْ تَكُوْنَ وَاثِقًا مِنْ قُدْرَتِكَ عَلَى الْفَوْزِ بِالسِّبَاقِ

You have to be confident in your ability to win the race

Write your own sentence below!

مُشْمَئِزٌّ
Disgusted by..

Singular (مُفْرَد)	مُشْمَئِزٌّ	مُشْمَئِزٌّ	مُشْمَئِزٌّ	مُشْمَئِزٌّ
Plural (جَمْع)	مُشْمَئِزُّونَ	مُشْمَئِزُّونَ	مُشْمَئِزُّونَ	مُشْمَئِزُّونَ

Sentence

قَالَ الْمُعَلِّمُ إِنَّنِي مُشْمَئِزٌّ مِنْ حُضُورِكَ إِلَى الْمَدْرَسَةِ هَذَا الْعَامِ

I am disgusted by your attendance at school this year, said the teacher

Write your own sentence below!

مُتَرَدِّدٌ
Hesitant

Singular (مُفْرَدٌ)	مُتَرَدِّدٌ	مُتَرَدِّدٌ	مُتَرَدِّدٌ	مُتَرَدِّدٌ
Plural (جَمْعٌ)	مُتَرَدِّدُوْنَ	مُتَرَدِّدُوْنَ	مُتَرَدِّدُوْنَ	مُتَرَدِّدُوْنَ

Sentence

لَا تَرَدَّدْ فِي أَفْعَالِكَ فَهَذَا يَدُلُّ عَلَى ضُعْفٍ

Don't be hesitant in your actions, as it shows weakness

Write your own sentence below!

هَادِئٌ
Calm

Singular (مُفْرَدٌ)	هَادِئٌ	هَادِئٌ	هَادِئٌ	هَادِئٌ
Plural (جَمْعٌ)	هَادِئُوْنَ	هَادِئُوْنَ	هَادِئُوْنَ	هَادِئُوْنَ

Sentence

كُنْ هَادِئًا ، لَا تَصْرَخْ فِي إِخْوَتِك

Be calm, don't shout at your siblings

Write your own sentence below!

مَشْغُوْلٌ
Busy

Singular (مُفْرَدٌ)	مَشْغُوْلٌ	مَشْغُوْلٌ	مَشْغُوْلٌ	مَشْغُوْلٌ
Plural (جَمْعٌ)	مَشْغُوْلُوْنَ	مَشْغُوْلُوْنَ	مَشْغُوْلُوْنَ	مَشْغُوْلُوْنَ

Sentence

أَنَا مَشْغُوْلٌ فِي عُطْلَةِ نِهَايَةِ الْأُسْبُوعِ، حَيْثُ أُحْضِرُ دُرُوْسًا خَاصَّةً

I am busy on the weekends, as I attend private classes

Write your own sentence below!

مَسْرُوْرٌ
Happy

Singular (مُفْرَدٌ)	مَسْرُوْرٌ	مَسْرُوْرٌ	مَسْرُوْرٌ	مَسْرُوْرٌ
Plural (جَمْعٌ)	مَسْرُوْرُوْنَ	مَسْرُوْرُوْنَ	مَسْرُوْرُوْنَ	مَسْرُوْرُوْنَ

Sentence

أَنَا مَسْرُوْرٌ بِلِقَائِكَ أَخِيْرًا بَعْدَ كُلِّ هَذِهِ السَّنَوَاتِ

I am happy to finally meet you after all of these years

Write your own sentence below!

شَخْصِيَّةٌ
Personality

Singular (مُفْرَدٌ)	شَخْصِيَّةٌ	شَخْصِيَّة	شَخْصِيَّة	شَخْصِيَّة
Plural (جَمْعٌ)	شَخْصِيَّاتٌ	شَخْصِيَات	شَخْصِيَات	شَخْصِيَات

Sentence

لَدَيَّ شَخْصِيَّةٌ خَجُولَةٌ وَمُتَحَفِّظَةٌ

I have a shy and reserved personality

Write your own sentence below!

عَاطِفٌ
Emotion

Singular (مُفْرَدٌ)	عَاطِفٌ	عَاطِفٌ	عَاطِفٌ	عَاطِفٌ
Plural (جَمْعٌ)	عَوَاطِفُ	عَوَاطِفُ	عَوَاطِفُ	عَوَاطِفُ

Sentence

كَانَتْ لَدَيَّ عَوَاطِفُ لَا تُوصَفُ عِنْدَمَا تَخَرَّجْتُ مِنَ الْجَامِعَةِ

I had indescribable emotions when I graduated from university

Write your own sentence below!

مُجَادَلَةٌ
Argument/Dispute

Singular (مُفْرَدٌ)	مُجَادَلَةٌ	مُجَادَلَةٌ	مُجَادَلَةٌ	مُجَادَلَةٌ
Plural (جَمْعٌ)	مُجَادَلَاتٌ	مُجَادَلَاتٌ	مُجَادَلَاتٌ	مُجَادَلَاتٌ

Sentence

إِنْدَلَعَتْ مُجَادَلَةٌ كَبِيرَةٌ بِسَبَبِ خِلَافٌ بَيْنَ الْمُوَظَّفِينَ

A big argument broke out because of a disagreement between the employees

Write your own sentence below!

فَخُوْرٌ
Proud

Singular (مُفْرَدٌ)	فَخُوْرٌ	فَخُوْرٌ	فَخُوْرٌ	فَخُوْرٌ
Plural (جَمْعٌ)	فَخُوْرُوْنَ	فَخُوْرُوْنَ	فَخُوْرُوْنَ	فَخُوْرُوْنَ

Sentence

لَا تَكُنْ فَخُوْرًا وَتَعْتَقِدُ أَنَّكَ أَفْضَلُ مِنَ الآخَرِيْنَ

Don't be prideful and think that you are better than the others

Write your own sentence below!

قَلِقٌ
Worried

Singular (مُفْرَدٌ)	قَلِقٌ	قَلِقٌ	قَلِقٌ	قَلِقٌ
Plural (جَمْعٌ)	قَلِقُوْنَ	قَلِقُوْنَ	قَلِقُوْنَ	قَلِقُوْنَ

Sentence

كَانَ أَنَسٌ قَلِقًا مِنْ عَدَمِ وُصُوْلِهِ إِلَى الْحَافِلَةِ فِي الْوَقْتِ الْمُحَدَّدِ

Anas was worried that he would not make the bus on time

Write your own sentence below!

مُتَضَايِقٌ
Uncomfortable

	Singular (مُفْرَدٌ)	مُتَضَايِقٌ	مُتَضَايِقٌ	مُتَضَايِقٌ	مُتَضَايِقٌ
	Plural (جَمْعٌ)	مُتَضَايِقُوْنَ	مُتَضَايِقُوْنَ	مُتَضَايِقُوْنَ	مُتَضَايِقُوْنَ

Sentence

كُنْتُ مُتَضَايِقٌ أَثْنَاءَ رِحْلَتِي إِلَى فَرَنْسَا

I was uncomfortable during my trip to France

Write your own sentence below!

خَائِفٌ
Afraid/Scared

Singular (مُفْرَدٌ)	خَائِفٌ	خَائِفٌ	خَائِفٌ	خَائِفٌ	خَائِفٌ
Plural (جَمْعٌ)	خَائِفُوْنَ	خَائِفُوْنَ	خَائِفُوْنَ	خَائِفُوْنَ	خَائِفُوْنَ

Sentence

كُنْتُ خَائِفٌ مِنْ الْكَوَابِيسِ عِنْدَمَا كُنْتُ صَغِيْرًا

I was afraid of nightmares when I was little

Write your own sentence below!

My final request...

Being a smaller author, reviews help me tremendously!
It would mean the world to me if you could leave a review.

If you liked reading this book and learned a thing or two, please let me know!

It only takes 30 seconds but means so much to me!

Thank you and I can't wait to see your thoughts.

Conclusion

I hope you have enjoyed this workbook; you should practice the words by writing them down repetitively on a separate notebook. You should have hopefully also picked up a ton of other vocabulary through the sentences that were displayed with each word.

If you are not sure how to use the word in a sentence yet, try to increase your vocabulary by learning and memorising more, I am sure that you will be able to use all of the words in your day-to-day life in no time!

Made in the USA
Las Vegas, NV
28 December 2023

83637497R10089